EAT YOUR GREENS

KALE, SPINACH, COLLARD GREENS, AND MORE

This edition published by Parragon Books Ltd in 2014 and distributed by

Parragon Inc.
440 Park Avenue South, 13th Floor
New York, NY 10016
www.parragon.com/lovefood

LOVE FOOD is an imprint of Parragon Books Ltd

ISBN 978-1-4723-6452-4

Printed in China

New recipes, introduction, and incidental text written by Christine McFadden
New photography by iangarlick.com
New food styling by Nikki Gee
Internal illustrations by Nicola O'Byrne
Project managed by Louisa Smith
Production controller: Joe Xavier

Notes for the Reader
This book uses standard kitchen measuring spoons and cups. All spoon and cup measurements are level unless otherwise indicated. Unless otherwise stated, milk is assumed to be whole, eggs are large, individual vegetables are medium, and pepper is freshly ground black pepper. Unless otherwise stated, all root vegetables should be peeled prior to using.

Garnishes, decorations, and serving suggestions are all optional and not necessarily included in the recipe ingredients or method. The times given are only an approximate guide. Preparation times differ according to the techniques used by different people and the cooking times may also vary from those given. Optional ingredients, variations, or serving suggestions have not been included in the time calculations.

Picture acknowledgments
The publisher would like to thank the following for the permission to reproduce copyright material: page 7 (radicchio) © Fuse/Getty Images; page 117 (tray of sodas in bottles) © Cultura/BRETT STEVENS/Getty Images.

CONTENTS

INTRODUCTION

Not so long ago, the thought of cooking and eating green vegetables would probably produce a sigh instead of a smile. How things have changed. Thanks to an ever-increasing choice of gorgeous greens in the stores and imaginative new ideas for ways of cooking them, not to mention the growing evidence pointing to their nutritional credentials, we are finally eating our greens. These once unloved vegetables are now the food heroes of the century and a green force to be reckoned with.

So what's so great about greens? Why do we need to eat them? First of all, as the recipes in this book prove, they taste fantastic. What's more, they're a breeze to cook and they're incredibly versatile—you can eat them raw or roasted, steamed or stir-fried, tossed into salads, made into a juice, packed into pancakes, or stirred into stews. Depending on what you serve them with, greens are as easy on the purse as they are on the waistline. But probably most importantly, they're packed with must-have nutrients that make you feel good. What's not to like?

KNOW YOUR GREENS

GREENS FOR COOKING
Kale

Impeccable nutritional credentials and stylish good looks have made kale a culinary superstar. Depending on the variety, the leaves are either flamboyantly frilled or deeply serrated. Some are a luminous blue-green contrasting with beautiful purple stems, while others are so dark they could almost be black. The flavor is satisfyingly rich and earthy, with a pleasant hint of sweetness. Kale is wonderfully versatile: steam, boil, sauté; braise with a grain; simmer in soups and stews; blend into pesto for pasta; or add young leaves to salads. For an addictive nibble, toss torn leaves with oil and roast in a low oven until crisp.

Spinach

There are two basic types of spinach: smooth-leaved, stem-free baby spinach for eating raw, and the larger puckered leaves (with stems) that are better cooked. Both have a melt-in-the-mouth texture, and an earthy, almost salty flavor. Spinach can be boiled, steamed, stir-fried, or wilted in butter or oil. It blends wonderfully with other ingredients—use it in pasta dishes, risotto, and as a pizza topping. Keep in mind that the leaves reduce by at least half once cooked.

Swiss chard

With Swiss chard, you get two vegetables in one: crunchy stems and melt-in-the-mouth leaves. The stems, which take longer to cook, make a tasty side dish and are good in a gratin or stir-fry. The leaves are used in the same way as spinach. Some varieties have spectacular technicolor stems and crinkly dark green leaves. One variety has broad white stems and smooth grass green leaves. The flavor is rich and earthy, similar to spinach but punchier.

Cabbage

Cabbages range from dense drumhead types and crinkly savoys to looser-leaved, conical spring cabbages and crisp napa cabbage. They come in a palette of colors: creamy pale yellow, luminous shades of green, and rich ruby red. Often underappreciated, cabbage is delicious lightly cooked, slowly braised, or shredded and served raw in a salad. The flavor ranges from mild and sweet spring cabbage and peppery red cabbage to the more challenging meatiness of the dense green varieties. For a side dish, steaming is preferable to boiling. Stir-frying and braising are good if you are after something more substantial. Fresh herbs lift the flavor, as does grated lemon zest and plenty of freshly ground black pepper.

Brussels sprouts

Brussels sprouts look like walnut-size cabbages. They are usually sold loose, but you can sometimes find them still attached to a long, rigid stem. Most are bright-green in color, although ruby red varieties also exist. Sprouts have a dense texture and a satisfyingly meaty, slightly sweet flavor. They are delicious lightly steamed, boiled, or stir-fried. Halve or quarter them if large, and cook until just tender—overcooked sprouts will disintegrate and smell unpleasant. Shredded finely, sprouts are surprisingly delicious eaten raw in coleslaw or a winter salad.

Roasted Broccoli with Pine Nuts & Parmesan (page 82)

Broccoli

Standard broccoli has a thick stem in the center and a single head of tightly packed florets of tiny unopened flower buds. Baby broccoli (also called Broccolini) has long, slender stems, with offshoots of thinner stems and leaves, and small purple or cream sprouting flower heads. Both have a meaty, full-bodied flavor. If not overcooked, standard broccoli has a crunchy texture, whereas baby broccoli is softer and chewier. Both types of broccoli are best steamed, stir-fried, or roasted instead of boiled—the texture is better and fewer nutrients are lost in the cooking water. Serve as a side dish or add small florets and sliced stems to risotto, pasta dishes, and thick tortilla-style omelets. Baby broccoli is delicious cooked in the same ways as asparagus—steamed or grilled—and anointed with olive oil or melted butter.

9

Tuna with Bok Choy & Soba Noodles (page 74)

Bok choy

One of the most delicious Asian greens, bok choy (also called pak choi) has edible ivory white stems and broad green leaves. Some varieties have thicker spoon-shape stems, and some have ruby red leaves. The stems are crisp and juicy with a hint of sweetness, while the leaves have a slight mustard tang. Bok choy is delicious both raw and cooked. Slice and add to salads, or use in stir-fries, soups, and noodle dishes. The stems take slightly longer to cook than the leaves.

Collard greens

Collard greens are an ancient type of leafy green, similar to kale. The paddle-shape leaves are green or blue-green with a fibrous stem. They need lengthy cooking to soften them, although shredding will speed things up. Their flavor is intensely cabbagelike with just a hint of bitterness. One of the most nutritionally rich vegetables, collard greens are good boiled, braised, or stir-fried, added to soups and stews, or stuffed and rolled like cabbage leaves. Discard the stem if it is particularly tough.

Mustard greens

Mustard greens are bracingly pungent—chew on some and you'll find your sinuses clear instantly. The leaves are striking—some are tinted purple-red with acid green stems, while others are completely green. Added sparingly, small young leaves add pep and color to a salad. Larger ones are best tamed by stir-frying. Asian seasonings, such as ginger, garlic, and chile, are good companions.

Turnip greens

Turnip greens come from varieties of turnip grown for their leaves instead of for their roots. They have thick stems and a strong, peppery flavor similar to that of mustard greens. Discard the stems, then slice the leaves into broad ribbons before cooking. Steam or boil until tender, or gently sauté them in butter or olive oil. Serve as a side dish, or add to soups and stews.

SALAD GREENS

Lettuce

Top of the lettuce league for crunch and full-bodied flavor is romaine—essential for the classic Caesar salad. High in crunch but low in flavor is iceberg—the bowl-shape leaves make a crisp wrapping for a tasty filling, and they are good shredded and served in a bun with burgers. Loose-headed butterhead has large soft leaves with a wonderful sweet flavor—perfect for a simple green salad. Smaller with a tightly packed heart, Boston is also excellent for green salads. Bronze-tinged red oak and frilly green-leaf lettuce add contrasting texture and color. Lettuce can also be used to make a vibrant soup or juice, or try it lightly braised with peas and new potatoes.

Chicory and endive

The chicory family includes frisée (curly endive), compact Belgian endive, and escarole (Batavia). Frisée has deeply serrated, slightly coarse leaves, while escarole leaves are smoother at the edges and softer. Both have dark green outer leaves and lemon yellow hearts. The flavor is sweet with just a hint of bitterness. Mixed with other greens, endives add crisp texture to a salad and are an excellent foil to rich meat dishes.

Arugula

Arugula has a distinctive peppery flavor and pleasantly chewy texture. Wild arugula has small, deeply notched, dark green leaves, while the more common variety has longer leaves with shallower notches. An essential green for Mediterranean-style salads, arugula can also be steamed or gently fried in oil and tossed with pasta.

Watercress

A feisty member of the Brassica family, watercress has a complex, peppery flavor. It is at its best served simply in a salad, perhaps with red onion slivers or shaved fennel, and it makes an excellent sandwich filling. Lightly wilted watercress is delicious tossed with pasta, or stirred into an omelet or a risotto. It also makes a vibrant green soup.

Radicchio

A round-headed member of the chicory family, radicchio has tightly furled, burgundy red leaves with white stems and veins. The slightly chewy leaves have a bittersweet flavor. They are best sliced and added sparingly to a salad. Radicchio is also good brushed with oil and grilled, or braised and added to risotto or pasta.

LIGHT BITES

RADICCHIO CAESAR SALAD

The classic Caesar salad is made with romaine lettuce, but here ruby red radicchio is used instead. Its bittersweet flavor goes well with the Parmesan, pancetta, and mustard dressing.

SERVES: 2　　　　**PREP TIME: 20 MINS**　　　　**COOK TIME: 5 MINS**

INGREDIENTS

4 thin slices pancetta

½ head of radicchio, tough outer leaves and coarse stems removed

2 cups prepared croutons

4 anchovies in oil, drained (optional)

¼ cup freshly grated Parmesan cheese, plus extra shavings to garnish

fresh basil leaves, to garnish

DRESSING

2 teaspoons lemon juice

1 teaspoon Dijon mustard

1 small garlic clove, crushed

dash of Worcestershire sauce

3 tablespoons extra virgin olive oil

salt and pepper, to taste

1. To make the dressing, combine the lemon juice, mustard, garlic, and Worcestershire sauce in a small bowl. Season with salt and pepper, then gradually whisk in the oil until thick.

2. Add the pancetta to a dry skillet and cook for 2–3 minutes, until crisp. Drain on paper towels. Break into bite-size pieces and set aside.

3. Tear the radicchio leaves into bite-size pieces. Place in a salad bowl with the croutons, anchovies (if using), and the grated Parmesan. Whisk the dressing, pour it over the greens, and toss to coat.

4. Top the salad with the reserved pancetta, the Parmesan shavings, and basil leaves. Serve immediately.

BABY BROCCOLI & RED CABBAGE SALAD

SERVES: 4   **PREP TIME: 15 MINS**   **COOK TIME: 15 MINS**

INGREDIENTS

1½ (6-ounce) packages baby broccoli

2½ cups shredded red cabbage

2 cooked beets in natural juices, drained and cut into matchsticks

2 tablespoons dried cranberries

3 tablespoons balsamic vinegar

CROUTONS

2 tablespoons olive oil

3 slices country-style whole-grain bread, torn into small pieces

1 tablespoon sunflower seeds

1 tablespoon flaxseed

1. Put the broccoli into the top of a steamer, cover, and set over a saucepan of simmering water. Steam for 3–5 minutes, or until tender. Cool under cold running water, cut the stems in half and the lower stems in half again lengthwise, then transfer to a salad bowl.

2. Add the red cabbage, beets, and dried cranberries to the salad bowl.

3. To make the croutons, heat the oil in a skillet over medium heat, add the bread, and cook for 3–4 minutes, stirring, until just beginning to brown. Add the sunflower seeds and flaxseed and cook for an additional 2–3 minutes, until lightly toasted.

4. Drizzle the balsamic vinegar over the salad and toss gently together. Sprinkle with the croutons and serve immediately.

HERO TIPS

The darker the broccoli florets—either purple, green, or deep blue-green—the higher the amounts of beta-carotene and vitamin C they contain.

SMOKED SALMON & PINK GRAPEFRUIT SALAD

SERVES: 2   **PREP TIME: 20 MINS**   **COOK TIME: NONE**

INGREDIENTS

1 pink grapefruit
2 cups arugula
2 cups frisée
½ fennel bulb, thinly sliced
large pinch of sea salt
1 tablespoon extra virgin olive oil, plus extra for drizzling
½ teaspoon white wine vinegar
2 ounces smoked salmon
pepper, to taste
cress or alfalfa sprouts, to garnish

1. Using a sharp knife, cut a slice from the top and bottom of the grapefruit. Remove the peel and white pith by cutting downward, following the shape of the fruit as closely as possible. Cut between the flesh and membrane of each segment and ease out the flesh. Discard the membrane and set aside the flesh.

2. Put the arugula, frisée, and fennel into a bowl. Sprinkle with the sea salt. Gently toss with your hands to distribute the salt. Add the oil and gently toss. Sprinkle with the vinegar, toss again, and divide between two serving plates.

3. Cut the smoked salmon into bite-size pieces and arrange on top of the salad with the grapefruit segments. Drizzle with oil and sprinkle with pepper.

4. Garnish with cress or sprouts and serve.

SEARED BEEF SALAD

A Thai-inspired salad with thinly sliced steak served over nutrient-boosting kale, sliced peppery radishes, and cool mint and cilantro, all drizzled with a zesty lime dressing.

SERVES: 4   **PREP TIME: 15 MINS**   **COOK TIME: 10 MINS**

INGREDIENTS

½ iceberg lettuce, leaves separated and torn into bite-size pieces

2 cups thinly sliced radishes

4 shallots, thinly sliced

1 cup shredded kale

2 tablespoons dried goji berries

½ cup coarsely chopped fresh mint

⅔ cup coarsely chopped fresh cilantro

2 tenderloin steaks, about 8 ounces each, visible fat removed

1 tablespoon sunflower oil

salt and pepper, to taste

DRESSING

juice of 1 lime

1 tablespoon soy sauce

3 tablespoons sunflower oil

1. Put the lettuce, radishes, and shallots into a serving bowl. Sprinkle the kale, goji berries, mint, and cilantro over them, then toss gently.

2. Preheat a ridged grill pan over high heat. Brush the steaks with the oil, then sprinkle with a little salt and pepper. Cook in the hot pan for 2 minutes on each side for medium-rare, 3 minutes for medium, or 4 minutes for well-done. Transfer the steaks to a plate and let rest for a few minutes.

3. Meanwhile, to make the dressing, put the lime juice, soy sauce, and oil in a clean screw-top jar, screw on the lid, and shake well. Drizzle the dressing over the salad, then toss together.

4. Divide the salad among four bowls. Thinly slice the steak and arrange it over the top, then serve immediately.

MIXED SALAD WITH PEANUT DRESSING

In this Indonesian-inspired salad, raw broccoli and cabbage are tossed with crunchy bean sprouts and cucumber and coated with a delicious peanut and soy dressing.

SERVES: 4   **PREP TIME: 20 MINS**   **COOK TIME: 5 MINS PLUS COOLING**

INGREDIENTS

2 cups small cauliflower florets

1½ cups small broccoli florets

1 cup shredded savoy cabbage

1½ cups fresh bean sprouts

1 cucumber, peeled, halved lengthwise, seeded, and thickly sliced

1 red bell pepper, seeded and finely chopped

DRESSING

2 tablespoons peanut oil

½ cup finely chopped unsalted peanuts

2 garlic cloves, finely chopped

2 tablespoons soy sauce

juice of 2 limes

½ red chile, seeded and finely chopped

1. Put the cauliflower, broccoli, cabbage, bean sprouts, cucumber, and red pepper into a salad bowl and toss gently.

2. To make the dressing, heat 1 tablespoon of the oil in a skillet over medium heat. Add the peanuts and garlic and stir-fry for 2–3 minutes, or until lightly browned. Remove from the heat and stir in the soy sauce, lime juice, chile, and the remaining oil, then let cool.

3. Spoon the dressing over the salad and toss gently. Divide among four bowls and serve immediately.

GREEN CREDENTIALS

Green vegetables boast an extraordinary range of health-promoting nutrients. Not only do they provide vitamins, minerals, and fiber, they're also packed with phytochemicals—a group of substances that make up a kind of anticarcinogenic cocktail that stimulates the body's defenses.

Among the most important substances are antioxidants. These include several minerals, vitamins C and E, and carotenoids (the plant version of vitamin A). Antioxidants protect the body by deactivating harmful free radicals that attack the nucleus of body cells, causing genetic changes that have been linked to cancer.

And that's not all. Green vegetables contain folate, a type of B vitamin needed for healthy red blood cells and especially important for growing children and pregnant women. They provide essential minerals, too, particularly those needed by women: calcium to help prevent osteoporosis (loss of bone mass) later in life, and iron to replace that lost in blood during menstruation. Just a few good reasons to eat your greens!

NUTRIENTS AND WHAT THEY DO:

Calcium

Strengthens the bones. Essential for muscle contraction, nerve function, enzyme activity, and blood clotting.

Iron

Involved in red blood cell production and transporting oxygen around the body.

Folate

A type of B vitamin vital for forming new cells and, therefore, essential for growing embryos. Also needed for normal development in children.

Vitamin A/Carotenoids

Vitamin A is found in food from animal sources, but it is also made from carotenoids in plant foods that convert to vitamin A in the body. Carotenoids are a group of substances that protect the cells, boost the immune system, and protect the skin from sun damage.

Vitamin C

Helps the body absorb iron from food. Also speeds up wound healing, helps keep skin supple, and boosts resistance to infection.

Important nutrients in greens (per 3½ ounces, raw)

	Calcium mg	Iron mg	Folate µg	Vitamin A iu	Vitamin C mg
Broccoli	47	0.73	63	623	89.2 (2nd)
Brussels sprouts	42	1.4	61	754	85 (3rd)
Lettuce, green leaf	36	0.86	38	2,666	9.2
Swiss chard	51	1.8 (2nd)	14	6,116	30
Collard greens	232 (1st)	0.47	129	5,019	35.3
Endive	52	0.83	142 (2nd)	2,167	6.5
Kale	150 (3rd)	1.47	141 (3rd)	9,990 (2nd)	120 (1st)
Watercress	120	0.20	9	3,191	43
Mustard greens	115	1.64 (3rd)	12	3,024	70
Cabbage	40	0.47	43	98	36.6
Spinach	99	2.71 (1st)	194 (1st)	9,377 (3rd)	28.1
Turnip greens	190 (2nd)	1.10	194 (1st)	11,587 (1st)	60
Bok choy	105	0.8	66	4,468	45

Sources: USDA database

 Vegetable containing the most of a particular nutrient

 Runners-up for each nutrient

PORK & COCONUT LETTUCE WRAPS

Crisp, bowl-shape leaves of iceberg or butterhead lettuce make a crunchy wrap for this spicy filling. Fold the leaves around the meat and eat with your fingers.

SERVES: 4　　　　**PREP TIME: 15 MINS**　　　**COOK TIME: 10 MINS**

INGREDIENTS

½ cup dried coconut chips

1 teaspoon fennel seeds

1 teaspoon cumin seeds

3 tablespoons coconut oil or vegetable oil

2 shallots, chopped

1 garlic clove, thinly sliced

¼–½ teaspoon crushed red pepper flakes

8 ounces fresh ground pork

juice of ½ lime

⅓ cup chopped fresh cilantro

8 large, crisp lettuce leaves, such as iceberg, thick stems removed

salt and pepper, to taste

finely sliced fresh red chile, to garnish

soy sauce and lime wedges, to serve

1. Preheat the oven to 350°F.

2. Spread the coconut chips on a baking sheet. Toast in the preheated oven for 2–3 minutes, until beginning to turn golden. Remove from the oven and set aside.

3. Place the fennel seeds and cumin seeds in a mortar and lightly crush with a pestle. Heat the oil in a skillet over medium–high heat. Add the shallots, garlic, crushed fennel and cumin seeds, and red pepper flakes and cook for 2 minutes, until just browned.

4. Stir in half of the coconut chips. Add the pork, breaking up any clumps with a fork, and cook for 3 minutes, until no longer pink. Stir in the lime juice and ¼ cup of the cilantro. Season with salt and pepper.

5. Divide the pork mixture among the lettuce leaves and arrange on a serving plate. Sprinkle with the remaining coconut chips and cilantro. Garnish with chile slices and serve immediately with a bowl of soy sauce for dipping and lime wedges for squeezing over the top.

TURKEY WRAPS WITH AVOCADO SALSA

SERVES: 4 **PREP TIME: 30 MINS PLUS MARINATING** **COOK TIME: 10 MINS**

INGREDIENTS

4 thin turkey breast cutlets (12 ounces in total)

olive oil, for brushing

4 romaine lettuce leaves, thick stems removed, leaves sliced into ribbons

4 corn tortillas, warmed

3 tablespoons sour cream

MARINADE

juice of 2 oranges

1 teaspoon cumin seeds, lightly crushed

½ teaspoon crushed red pepper flakes

4 tablespoons olive oil

salt and pepper, to taste

SALSA

2 avocados, peeled, pitted, and diced

1 small red onion, diced

2 tomatoes, seeded and diced

2 tablespoons chopped fresh cilantro

juice of 1 lime

1. Slice the turkey into 1½ x 2½-inch strips. Place them in a shallow dish.

2. To make the marinade, whisk together all the marinade ingredients. Pour it over the turkey, cover, and marinate in the refrigerator for 4 hours or overnight. Remove from the refrigerator at least 30 minutes before cooking to bring the turkey to room temperature.

3. To make the salsa, combine all the ingredients in a small bowl.

4. Preheat the broiler to high. Drain the turkey, discarding the marinade. Thread the strips accordion-style onto metal skewers (or use wooden skewers with aluminum foil wrapped around the ends so that they don't burn) and brush with oil. Place the skewers on a rack in the broiler pan and cook under the preheated broiler for about 5 minutes on each side, until the turkey is cooked through and starting to brown at the edges. Remove the turkey from the skewers, set aside, and keep warm.

5. Divide the lettuce among the tortillas and arrange the turkey on top. Add a little sour cream and salsa. Roll the bottoms and sides of the tortillas over the filling and serve immediately.

2

3

4

ARUGULA, WHITE BEAN & TOMATO BRUSCHETTA

In this dish, crisp toasted sourdough is topped with peppery arugula, quartered tomatoes, and an addictive mixture of crushed beans, garlic, and herbs. It's easy to make and hard to beat as a snack or appetizer.

SERVES: 4   **PREP TIME: 20 MINS**   **COOK TIME: 5 MINS**

INGREDIENTS

2 (15-ounce) cans cannellini beans, drained and rinsed

1 garlic clove, crushed

2 tablespoons extra virgin olive oil, plus extra for drizzling

1 teaspoon lemon juice

1 tablespoon chopped fresh flat-leaf parsley

¾ teaspoon chopped fresh rosemary leaves

1 cup arugula leaves

8–10 slices sourdough bread

16–20 baby plum tomatoes, quartered lengthwise

sea salt and pepper, to taste

1. Combine the beans, garlic, oil, lemon juice, parsley, and rosemary in a large bowl. Season with sea salt and pepper, then mash to a chunky puree with a fork.

2. Preheat the broiler to medium. Coarsely chop the arugula leaves if large.

3. Place the bread under the preheated broiler and toast on both sides.

4. Thickly spread the bread with the bean puree. Pile the arugula on top, followed by the tomato quarters. Sprinkle with sea salt and pepper, drizzle with a little oil, and serve immediately.

BUCKWHEAT PANCAKES WITH SPINACH & FETA

MAKES: 8

PREP TIME: 30 MINS PLUS RESTING

COOK TIME: 45 MINS

INGREDIENTS

½ cup buckwheat flour

⅓ cup all-purpose flour

2 eggs, lightly beaten

1½ cups milk

2 tablespoons butter, plus extra for frying

2 cups halved or thickly sliced cremini mushrooms

3 (6-ounce) packages baby spinach

¼ cup coarsely chopped walnuts

⅓ cup crumbled feta cheese

large pinch of freshly grated nutmeg

large pinch of crushed red pepper flakes

salt and pepper, to taste

snipped fresh chives, to garnish

1. Sift together the buckwheat flour, all-purpose flour, and ½ teaspoon salt into a large bowl. Make a well in the center and drop in the eggs. Using a fork, mix in some of the flour from the edge of the bowl. Gradually add the milk, stirring to a smooth batter. Set aside for 30 minutes, then melt the butter in a small saucepan and whisk it into the batter.

2. Melt a pat of butter in a large skillet, add the mushrooms, and sauté for 5 minutes. Remove from the heat and set aside.

3. Meanwhile, steam the spinach for 4 minutes. Drain, squeezing out as much liquid as possible, then coarsely chop. Add the walnuts and feta to the mushrooms and mix well. Add the spinach, nutmeg, and red pepper flakes, and season with salt and pepper. Keep warm over low heat.

4. Add a pat of butter to a 9½-inch nonstick skillet and place over medium heat until sizzling. Pour in ¼ cup of the batter, rotating the pan to distribute evenly. Cook for 2–2½ minutes on each side, turning carefully, until flecked with brown. Set aside and keep warm while you cook seven more pancakes in the same way.

5. Spoon some of the filling down the middle of each pancake. Roll up, then slice in half. Garnish with chives and serve immediately.

STEAK SANDWICHES WITH CARAMELIZED ONIONS

SERVES: 4   **PREP TIME: 15 MINS**   **COOK TIME: 50 MINS**

INGREDIENTS

2 tenderloin steaks
(about 8 ounces each)

2 red onions, sliced into
thick rings

3 tablespoons olive oil, plus
extra for brushing and
drizzling

2 teaspoons sugar

2 teaspoons balsamic vinegar

8 slices sourdough bread

1 beefsteak tomato, sliced

2 cups arugula

salt and pepper, to taste

1. Preheat the oven to 375°F.

2. Lightly brush the steaks with oil, sprinkle with salt and pepper, and set aside at room temperature.

3. Put the onion rings in a large bowl with the oil and sugar, season with salt and pepper, and toss well, separating the rings. Spread out in a roasting pan. Roast in the preheated oven for 20–25 minutes, stirring every 10 minutes, until just beginning to brown. Sprinkle with the vinegar, stir, and spread out. Roast for an additional 5–8 minutes, until brown and sticky. Transfer to a bowl and set aside.

4. Heat a ridged grill pan over medium–high heat. Add the steaks and cook for 3–3½ minutes on each side. Transfer to a board and let rest for 5 minutes. Preheat the broiler to medium.

5. Place the bread under the preheated broiler and toast on both sides. Arrange the tomato slices and arugula on four of the toast slices. Drizzle with a little oil and sprinkle with salt and pepper.

6. Carve each steak diagonally into ¾-inch slices. Arrange on top of the arugula, then add a few caramelized onion rings (store any leftover onions in an airtight container in the refrigerator for up to one month). Top with the remaining toast slices and serve immediately.

GET FRESH!

Nowadays we have a choice of places to buy green vegetables, from supermarkets and convenience stores to farmer's markets, farm shops, and vegetable boxes from CSA farms, to name a few. Supermarkets probably provide the widest choice, usually with year-round availability. Much of the produce is packaged, prewashed, and already prepared—a great convenience if you lead an action-packed life.

How long will my greens last?

Regardless of whether you buy greens packaged or loose, there is no knowing how long they will last once you get them home. Packaged greens may be marked with a 'best if used by (or before)' date, but that doesn't mean they will stay fresh until then (or won't be fresh after that date). So it makes sense to understand what to look for in terms of freshness, and, equally important, to know how to store your greens once you get them back home.

What's the best way of storing greens?

Keep all your greens in the refrigerator salad drawer in a brown paper bag or a ventilated plastic bag. This provides the slightly humid but well-ventilated atmosphere that they need. A sealed plastic bag is better for watercress and fragile leafy greens that need an enclosed, moist environment.

How do I know they are fresh?

In general, greens should be full of crispness and bounce, particularly the leafy types.

Broccoli

Look for bright green heads. Avoid any that are flabby, yellowing, or cracked at the cut end of the stem. Choose baby broccoli with undamaged florets.

Brussels sprouts

Look for firm, tightly packed buds. Don't buy them if the outer leaves are yellow or limp.

Cabbage

Choose heads that feel heavy with crisp leaves. Reject any with yellowing outer leaves, or if the outer leaves have been stripped.

Swiss chard, collard greens, kale, and bok choy

Look for crisp, fresh leaves and firm stems. Don't buy if the leaves are limp or yellowing or the stems are bruised.

Spinach and turnip greens

Look for dewy-fresh, dark green leaves. Skip them if they are bruised, yellowing, or slimy.

Lettuce, chicory, endive, and mustard greens

Look for dewy-fresh leaves and firm centers for hearting lettuces. Don't buy any with brown or slimy leaves.

Radicchio

Look for tightly packed, firm heads. Don't buy them if the outer leaves have been removed.

Arugula and watercress

Look for sprightly, bright green leaves. Skip them if they appear to be yellowing or slimy.

KALE & POTATO CAKES WITH FRIED EGGS

SERVES: 4　　　**PREP TIME: 30 MINS**　　　**COOK TIME: 35 MINS**

INGREDIENTS

4 russet potatoes, unpeeled, cut into large chunks

4 ounces kale, thick stems removed (about 2 cups prepared)

large pat of butter

4 scallions, some green included, finely chopped

2 teaspoons dill seeds

1 teaspoon finely grated lemon zest

⅓ cup vegetable oil

4 eggs

salt and pepper, to taste

1. Put the potatoes in a large saucepan of lightly salted water. Bring to a boil and cook for 15–20 minutes, until tender but not disintegrating.

2. Meanwhile, bring a separate saucepan of water to a boil. Add the kale and blanch for 2 minutes. Drain and rinse under cold running water, squeezing out as much liquid as possible, then coarsely chop.

3. Drain the potatoes, then return them to the pan for a few minutes to dry. Mash with the butter and season with salt and pepper.

4. Combine the potatoes, kale, scallions, dill seeds, and lemon zest in a large bowl, mixing well with a fork. Season with salt and pepper and shape into four ½-inch-thick patties.

5. Heat 3 tablespoons of the oil in a large, nonstick skillet over medium heat. Add the patties and cook for 3–3½ minutes on each side, turning carefully, until golden. Set aside and keep warm.

6. Heat the remaining oil in the pan, break in the eggs, and cook until done to your liking. Place a fried egg on top of each patty. Serve immediately.

SPINACH & PINE NUT FRITTATA

SERVES: 4　　　　　**PREP TIME: 20 MINS**　　　**COOK TIME: 20 MINS**

INGREDIENTS

1½ (6-ounce) packages baby spinach

1 tablespoon vegetable oil

2 tablespoons butter

1 large shallot, halved lengthwise and finely sliced

1 garlic clove, thinly sliced

⅓ cup pine nuts, toasted

¼ teaspoon crushed red pepper flakes

8 eggs

¼ cup freshly grated Parmesan cheese

salt and pepper, to taste

leafy green salad, to serve

1. Wash the spinach thoroughly. Drain and put into a saucepan without any extra water. Cover and cook over medium heat for 5 minutes, stirring occasionally, until just tender. Drain, squeezing out as much liquid as possible, then coarsely chop.

2. Heat the oil and butter in a 9½-inch nonstick skillet over medium heat. Add the shallot and sauté for 3 minutes, until translucent. Add the garlic and sauté for an additional 2 minutes. Stir in the spinach, pine nuts, and red pepper flakes. Season with salt and pepper.

3. Beat the eggs in a small bowl with the Parmesan. Pour into the pan, stirring to distribute the spinach evenly. Cover and cook over medium–low heat for 5–7 minutes, until almost set. Meanwhile, preheat the broiler to medium.

4. Place the pan under the preheated broiler for 1–2 minutes to finish cooking the top of the frittata. Slice into wedges and serve with a leafy green salad.

HERO TIPS

It's important to use a 9½-inch skillet. If the pan is bigger, the egg mixture won't be deep enough to submerge the vegetables.

LENTIL & COLLARD GREENS SOUP

SERVES: 6   **PREP TIME: 20 MINS**   **COOK TIME: 1 HR**

INGREDIENTS

¾ cup brown lentils

1 onion, finely diced

1¾ cups tomato sauce

4½–5 cups chicken stock or vegetable stock

½ teaspoon cumin seeds, lightly crushed, plus extra to garnish

12 ounces collard greens (about 12 cups prepared)

3 small potatoes, cut into ½-inch cubes

⅓ cup chopped fresh mint

2 whole-wheat pita breads

⅓ cup Greek-style yogurt

salt and pepper, to taste

lemon wedges, to garnish

1. Put the lentils in a large saucepan with the onion, tomato sauce, 3½ cups of the stock, the cumin seeds, and ½ teaspoon salt. Bring to a boil, then cover and simmer over low heat for 20 minutes, until the lentils are just tender.

2. Trim the collard greens and very thinly slice the leaves widthwise.

3. Add the potatoes to the lentils and cook for 10 minutes.

4. Add the collard greens and cook for an additional 20 minutes. If necessary, add the remaining stock to thin the soup—but it should still be thick. Stir in ¼ cup of the mint and season with salt and pepper.

5. Meanwhile, preheat the broiler to medium. Open out the pita breads and toast under the preheated broiler for 3 minutes, until crisp. Break into bite-size pieces and arrange around the edge of six soup bowls.

6. Ladle the soup into the bowls. Add 1 tablespoon of yogurt to each and sprinkle with the remaining mint and cumin seeds. Garnish with lemon wedges and serve immediately.

LEEK, POTATO & SPINACH SOUP

SERVES: 4   **PREP TIME: 15 MINS**   **COOK TIME: 40 MINS**

INGREDIENTS

2 tablespoons butter

2 leeks, halved lengthwise and thinly sliced

2 potatoes, cut into bite-size chunks

1 (10-ounce) package fresh spinach, trimmed and leaves sliced

1¼ cups vegetable stock

1 teaspoon lemon juice

pinch of freshly grated nutmeg

salt and pepper, to taste

sour cream, to serve

1. Melt the butter in a large saucepan over low–medium heat. Add the leeks and potatoes, cover, and cook gently for 10 minutes, or until beginning to soften.

2. Stir in 7 cups of the spinach. Cover and cook for 2–3 minutes, until starting to wilt. Season with salt and pepper. Stir in half the stock. Bring to a boil, then simmer, partly covered, for 20 minutes.

3. Transfer half the soup to a food processor and process until smooth. Return to the pan.

4. Puree the remaining uncooked spinach and stock. Add to the soup in the pan. Stir in the lemon juice and nutmeg and gently reheat.

5. Ladle into bowls, swirl in a spoonful of sour cream, and serve immediately.

HERO TIPS

If you'd prefer a smooth soup, transfer all the soup to the food processor in step 3 and process until smooth. You may need to do this in batches.

CREAM OF ARUGULA SOUP

SERVES: 6　　　　**PREP TIME: 20 MINS**　　　**COOK TIME: 55 MINS**

INGREDIENTS

1 tablespoon butter

1 large onion, halved and sliced

2 leeks, sliced

6⅓ cups vegetable stock

½ cup white rice

2 carrots, sliced

3 garlic cloves, peeled

1 bay leaf

2 soft, round lettuce, cored and coarsely chopped

¾ cup heavy cream

freshly grated nutmeg, to taste

3 cups coarsely chopped arugula, plus extra leaves to garnish

salt and pepper, to taste

1. Melt the butter in a large saucepan over medium heat and add the onion and leeks. Cover and cook, stirring frequently, for 3–4 minutes, until the vegetables begin to soften.

2. Add the stock, rice, carrots, garlic, and bay leaf with a large pinch of salt. Bring just to a boil, then reduce the heat, cover, and simmer for 25–30 minutes, or until the rice and vegetables are tender. Remove and discard the bay leaf.

3. Add the lettuce to the saucepan and cook, stirring occasionally, for 10 minutes, until the leaves are wilted.

4. Remove the saucepan from the heat and let cool slightly. Transfer to a food processor or blender, in batches if necessary, and process until smooth.

5. Return the soup to the rinsed-out pan and reheat gently; do not boil. Stir in the cream and season with nutmeg. Simmer, stirring occasionally, for 5 minutes, until warmed through.

6. Add the arugula and simmer, stirring occasionally, for 2–3 minutes, until wilted. Taste and adjust the seasoning, adding salt and pepper if needed. Ladle the soup into warm bowls, top each serving with a few arugula leaves, and serve immediately.

DYNAMIC DINNERS

KALE, LEMON & CHIVE LINGUINE

SERVES: 2-3   **PREP TIME: 20 MINS**   **COOK TIME: 20 MINS**

INGREDIENTS

9 ounces kale, thick stems removed, leaves sliced widthwise into thin ribbons (about 3¾ cups prepared)

8 ounces dried linguine

½ cup olive oil

1 onion, chopped

1 garlic clove, thinly sliced

grated zest of 1 large lemon

large pinch of dried red pepper flakes

3 tablespoons snipped fresh chives

¼ cup freshly grated Parmesan cheese

salt and pepper, to taste

1. Bring a large saucepan of water to a boil. Add the kale and blanch for 2 minutes, until just wilted. Drain, reserving the water, and set aside.

2. Bring the reserved water to a boil in the large pan. Add the linguine and cook according to package directions until tender but still firm to the bite.

3. Meanwhile, heat the oil in a large skillet over medium–high heat. Add the onion and sauté for 2–3 minutes, until translucent. Add the garlic and sauté for an additional minute.

4. Stir in the kale, lemon zest, and red pepper flakes and season with salt and pepper. Cook over medium heat for 4–5 minutes, stirring occasionally, until tender but still bright green. Add a little of the cooking water if the mixture becomes dry.

5. Drain the pasta and transfer to a warm serving dish. Add the kale mixture, tossing with the pasta to mix. Stir in the chives and Parmesan and season with salt and pepper. Toss again and serve immediately.

HERO TIPS

Using the kale cooking water to cook the pasta not only saves time and fuel, but also gives the pasta more flavor.

SPICY EGGPLANT & CHICKPEA CASSEROLE

This hearty Middle Eastern-style vegetarian stew is packed with rich, spicy flavors. Shredded green cabbage is added toward the end of cooking so that it keeps its vibrant color.

SERVES: 4-6   **PREP TIME: 25 MINS**   **COOK TIME: 55 MINS**

INGREDIENTS

¼ cup olive oil

1 large onion, chopped

1 tablespoon cumin seeds, crushed

½ teaspoon allspice berries, crushed

2 garlic cloves, thinly sliced

1 large red bell pepper, seeded and cut into 1-inch pieces

2 eggplant, thickly sliced and cut into segments

2 (15-ounce) cans chickpeas, drained and rinsed

1 (14½-ounce) can diced tomatoes

2 cups vegetable stock

½ head of cabbage, tough stems removed

salt and pepper, to taste

cooked quinoa, to serve

1. Heat the oil in a 4-quart Dutch oven or flameproof casserole dish. Add the onion, spices, ½ teaspoon salt, and ¼ teaspoon pepper. Cook over medium–high heat for 5 minutes, until the onion is soft but not browned.

2. Add the garlic, red bell pepper, and eggplant and cook for an additional 5 minutes, until the red bell pepper and eggplant are beginning to soften.

3. Stir in the chickpeas, tomatoes, and stock. Bring to a boil, then reduce the heat and simmer, covered, for 30 minutes.

4. Meanwhile, slice the cabbage leaves into ribbons. Add the cabbage to the casserole, cover, and simmer for 10–12 minutes, until the cabbage is tender but still bright green. Taste and adjust the seasoning, adding salt and pepper, if needed. Serve immediately with cooked quinoa.

SWISS CHARD & RICOTTA PHYLLO PIE

MAKES: 9   **PREP TIME: 30 MINS**   **COOK TIME: 55 MINS**

INGREDIENTS

2 pounds rainbow Swiss chard
4 tablespoons butter
2 leeks, sliced
2 garlic cloves, thinly sliced
3 tablespoons chopped mixed
fresh herbs, such as
thyme, marjoram, and
flat-leaf parsley
1⅔ cups ricotta cheese
⅔ cup freshly grated
Parmesan cheese
pinch of freshly grated nutmeg
2 eggs, beaten
12 large sheets phyllo pastry
olive oil, for brushing
½ cup pine nuts
salt and pepper, to taste

1. Chop the Swiss chard stems into chunks. Slice the leaves into thin ribbons.

2. Heat the butter in a large skillet over medium heat. Add the leeks and Swiss chard stems, cover, and sauté for 5–7 minutes, until soft. Add the Swiss chard leaves, garlic, and herbs. Cover and gently sauté until the leaves are tender. Transfer the vegetables to a colander and drain.

3. Beat together the ricotta, Parmesan, nutmeg, and eggs in a large bowl. Mix in the drained vegetables. Season with salt and pepper.

4. Preheat the oven to 375°F. Place one sheet of the phyllo pastry in an oiled 9 x 12-inch roasting pan, trimming to fit. Brush with oil and sprinkle with a few pine nuts. Add five more sheets of pastry, lightly brushing each with oil and sprinkling with more pine nuts.

5. Pour in the filling and cover with five more sheets of phyllo pastry, brushing each sheet with oil and sprinkling with pine nuts. Add the final sheet and brush with oil. Using a sharp knife, cut through all the layers to make nine 3-inch squares.

6. Bake in the preheated oven for 35–40 minutes, until golden and crisp. Cut into squares again and serve hot or at room temperature.

KALE & FAVA BEAN CASSEROLE

SERVES: 6 **PREP TIME: 25 MINS PLUS SOAKING** **COOK TIME: 2 HRS**

INGREDIENTS

2⅓ cups dried fava beans, soaked overnight

1 tablespoon cumin seeds

2 teaspoons dried oregano

3 tablespoons peanut oil

2 onions, chopped

2 garlic cloves, thinly sliced

1–3 fresh red or green chiles, seeded and sliced

1 (14½-ounce) can diced tomatoes

2 cups vegetable stock

3 cups trimmed and shredded kale

⅓ cup chopped fresh cilantro

juice of 1 lime

salt and pepper, to taste

TO GARNISH

2 avocados, peeled, pitted, and diced

1 small red onion, halved and thinly sliced

1. Drain the beans, put them into a large saucepan, and cover with water. Boil rapidly for 15 minutes, then reduce the heat and simmer for 30–45 minutes, until tender but not disintegrating. Drain and set aside.

2. Put the cumin seeds into a small dry skillet over medium heat and cook until fragrant. Add the oregano and cook for a few seconds, then immediately remove from the pan. Lightly crush the mixture in a mortar with a pestle.

3. Heat the oil in a large Dutch oven or flameproof casserole dish over medium heat. Add the onions and spice-and-herb mixture. Sauté for 5 minutes, until the onions are translucent. Add the garlic and chiles and sauté for an additional 2 minutes.

4. Stir in the tomatoes, beans, and stock. Season with salt and pepper and bring to a boil. Reduce the heat, cover, and simmer for 30 minutes, stirring occasionally.

5. Increase the heat and stir in the kale. Simmer, uncovered, for 7 minutes, or until tender but still brightly colored. Stir in the cilantro and lime juice.

6. Ladle into soup bowls and garnish with the avocado and red onion. Serve immediately.

GREENS, PEA & BEAN BURGERS

A mixture of peppery greens adds color and nutrients to these mouthwatering veggie burgers. They are light yet flavorful—even meat-eaters will gobble them up.

MAKES: 8

PREP TIME: 30 MINS PLUS STANDING

COOK TIME: 25 MINS

INGREDIENTS

4 cups peppery salad greens, such as arugula, mustard greens, bok choy (green part only), or a mixture, thick stems removed

⅓ cup cooked peas, mashed

1 (15-ounce) can lima beans, drained, rinsed and mashed

1 tablespoon grated onion

1½ tablespoons chopped fresh mint

¼ teaspoon salt

pinch of pepper

1 egg, beaten

1 cup stale bread crumbs

3 tablespoons vegetable oil

TO SERVE

4 pita breads, halved

cherry tomatoes, halved

mayonnaise

1. Coarsely slice the salad greens. Steam them for 3 minutes, then drain and rinse under cold running water, squeezing out as much liquid as possible.

2. Combine the cooked greens with the peas, beans, onion, mint, salt, pepper, and egg. Mix thoroughly with a fork. Stir in the bread crumbs, mixing well. Let stand at room temperature for 30 minutes.

3. Divide the mixture into eight ½-inch-thick patties, each 2½ inches in diameter, firming the edges well.

4. Heat the oil in a nonstick skillet over medium–high heat. Working in batches, add the patties and cook for 2½–3 minutes on each side, turning carefully, until golden and crisp. Meanwhile, preheat the broiler to medium.

5. Toast the pita bread halves under the preheated broiler. Stuff each half with a bean patty, cherry tomato halves, and a spoonful of mayonnaise. Serve immediately.

58

TURNIP GREENS & RICOTTA CANNELLONI

SERVES: 4   **PREP TIME: 45 MINS**   **COOK TIME: 1 HR 30 MINS**

INGREDIENTS

12 ounces turnip greens, trimmed (about 12 cups prepared)

1¾ cups ricotta cheese

finely grated zest of 1 lemon

1 teaspoon fresh thyme leaves

¼ teaspoon freshly grated nutmeg

½ cup freshly grated Parmesan cheese

small handful of fresh basil leaves, torn, plus extra leaves to garnish

12 cannelloni tubes, cooked according to package directions and drained

salt and pepper, to taste

SAUCE

2 (14½-ounce) cans diced tomatoes

2 onions, quartered

4 tablespoons butter

1 cup chicken stock or vegetable stock

salt and pepper, to taste

1. To make the sauce, put the tomatoes, onions, and butter into a saucepan over medium heat. Simmer, uncovered, for 45 minutes, stirring occasionally. Strain to remove the onion, then return to the pan. Stir in the stock, season with salt and pepper, then set aside and keep warm.

2. Meanwhile, preheat the oven to 350°F. Stack the turnip greens and slice them into very thin ribbons. Steam for 5 minutes, until just tender. Drain and rinse under cold running water, squeezing out as much liquid as possible.

3. Mix the turnip greens with the ricotta, lemon zest, thyme, and nutmeg. Add half the Parmesan and the torn basil and season with salt and pepper. Stuff the mixture into the cannelloni tubes, packing it in well.

4. Spoon half the sauce over the bottom of an ovenproof dish large enough to hold the cannelloni tubes in a single layer. Arrange the cannelloni tubes on top and spoon over the remaining sauce. Sprinkle with the remaining Parmesan.

5. Cover with aluminum foil and bake in the preheated oven for 25–35 minutes, until cooked through. Garnish with basil and serve immediately.

PREPARE FOR SUCCESS!

To serve greens at their best with maximum flavor and nutrients, it's well worth learning a few tricks of the trade.

Cabbage

Trim the bottom and separate the outer leaves. Cut out the tough stem in the leaf by slicing up each side of it into the leaf. For wedges, quarter the cabbage lengthwise, leaving the core in the center attached so the leaves don't separate. For shredded cabbage, cut out the core and slice the quarters widthwise into ribbons.

Don't waste the core—it is flavorsome and crunchy. Slice it thinly and add to salads or serve as a crudité with good mayonnaise or a mustard vinaigrette.

Swiss chard

To separate the stems from the leaves, lay the leaf flat and slice up each side of the stem into the leaf. Slice or dice the stems according to the recipe. Slice the leaves into wide ribbons. Remember that they dramatically reduce in bulk when cooked.

Salad greens

Dunk leaves in cold water, then drain well and dry in a salad spinner. Spread out between layers of paper towels to blot up remaining moisture. Salad greens should be perfectly dry, otherwise the dressing won't cling to the leaves. To avoid bruising, tear salad greens instead of cutting them with a knife.

Broccoli

Cut a standard head of broccoli into florets, leaving about 1 inch of stem attached. If the florets are large, slice them lengthwise into two or three even pieces so they all take the same amount of time to cook. Remember that the stem in the center is as tasty as the florets. Peel it and slice widthwise into thin disks. Cook with the florets or stir-fry separately.

To prepare baby broccoli, strip the larger lower leaves from the main stem. If the stem seems tough, pull the end of the stem toward the tip until it snaps, then discard the end. Cut off the flower heads, leaving about 3¼ inches of the stem and surrounding tender leaves attached. You can halve the stem lengthwise if it is thick.

Kale and collard greens

To remove tough stems, stack a few leaves on top of each other, aligning the stems in the center. Fold the stack in half along the stems. Using a long, sharp knife, remove the stems with a single stroke of the knife. Alternatively, hold a folded leaf in one hold, grasp the stem with the other, and strip it away.

Bok choy

To prepare bok choy, cut off the bottom and pull the densely packed leaves apart. Wash in several changes of water to remove any grit. The fleshy ends take longer to cook, so if you are using bok choy in a stir-fry, cook the ends first and add the leaves later. However, tender baby bok choy can be cooked whole.

Brussels sprouts

Remove any damaged or discolored outer leaves. Trim the bottom but not right up to the leaves, otherwise they'll fall off during cooking. There is no need to cut an X into the bottom of each—doing so allows water to penetrate further into the sprouts, making them soggy.

ROASTED CHICKEN WITH WATERCRESS BUTTER

SERVES: 4   **PREP TIME: 30 MINS**   **COOK TIME: 1 HR 50 MINS PLUS RESTING**

INGREDIENTS

1 bunch of watercress, leaves picked from the stems

1 stick unsalted butter, at room temperature

finely grated zest and juice of 1 small orange

2 tablespoons finely chopped shallot

½ teaspoon black peppercorns, crushed

a large pinch of sea salt

1 (3¼-pound) chicken

1¾ cups chicken stock

all-purpose flour, for sprinkling

salt and pepper, to taste

1. Preheat the oven to 400°F.

2. Chop the watercress and mix with the butter, orange zest, shallot, peppercorns, and sea salt.

3. Loosen the chicken skin by pushing your fingers underneath. Insert the watercress butter under the skin, smoothing it to the shape of the bird.

4. Place the chicken, breast-side down, in a roasting pan. Add ⅓–½ cup of the stock, then roast in the preheated oven for 20 minutes.

5. Turn the chicken over and reduce the oven temperature to 350°F. Roast for an additional 1 hour 15 minutes, basting occasionally, until the juices run clear when the tip of a sharp knife is inserted into the thickest part of the meat (in the inner thigh area near the breast). Transfer the chicken to a warm serving plate and let rest for 10 minutes.

6. Pour away most of the fat from the pan. Sprinkle the juices with a little flour and stir over medium heat, scraping up the sediment from the bottom of the pan. Stir in the orange juice, the remaining stock, and any juices that have flowed from the chicken. Bring to a boil, stirring. Season with salt and pepper. Strain the gravy into a gravy boat and serve immediately with the chicken.

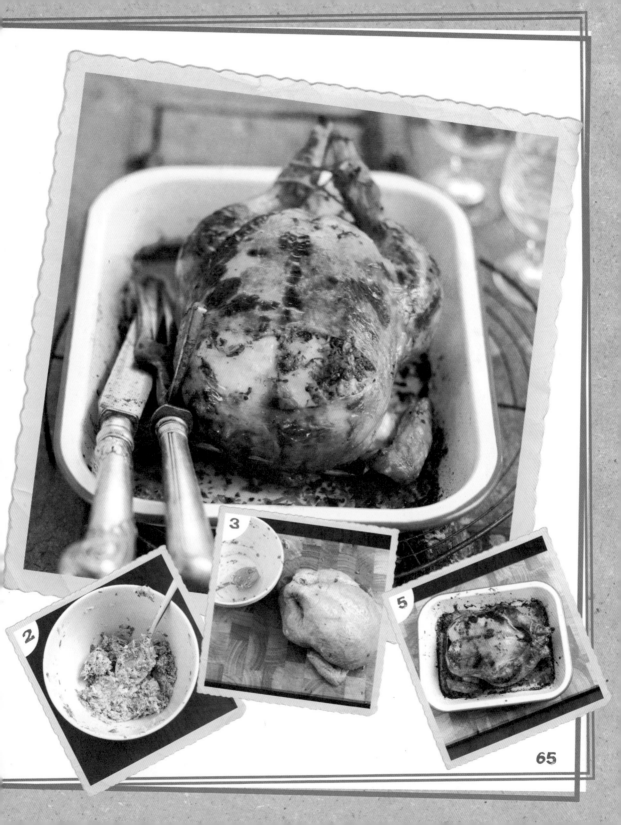

RED CABBAGE, TURKEY & QUINOA PILAF

Red cabbage comes into its own here, adding rich color to this magnificent dish. Cranberries and Brazil nuts add flavor and crunch, while quinoa provides a moist and fluffy base.

SERVES: 4-6   **PREP TIME: 30 MINS**   **COOK TIME: 55 MINS**

INGREDIENTS

- ½ cup white quinoa
- ½ cup red quinoa
- ¼ cup vegetable oil
- 1 large red onion, halved and sliced
- 1 teaspoon cumin seeds, crushed
- 4-inch cinnamon stick, broken
- ½ head of red cabbage, core removed, leaves sliced into ribbons
- 1–1½ cups chicken stock or vegetable stock
- 2½ cups bite-size, cooked turkey pieces
- 2 carrots, shaved into ribbons
- ½ cup dried cranberries
- ½ cup coarsely chopped Brazil nuts
- salt and pepper, to taste
- small handful of fresh flat-leaf parsley leaves, to garnish

1. Combine the white quinoa and red quinoa, then place in a strainer and rinse under cold running water. Put in a saucepan with ½ teaspoon salt and enough water to cover by ⅝ inch. Bring to a boil, cover, and simmer over low heat for 15 minutes. Remove from the heat but keep the pan covered for 5 minutes to let the grains swell. Fluff up the grains with a fork and set aside.

2. Heat the oil in a large skillet over medium–high heat. Add the onion with the spices and ½ teaspoon salt and sauté for 5 minutes, until the onion is soft but not browned.

3. Add the cabbage, 1 cup of the stock, and ¼ teaspoon pepper. Cover and cook over medium heat for 15–20 minutes, until the cabbage is just tender. Add the turkey, carrots, cranberries, and Brazil nuts. Cook, uncovered, for 5 minutes, until the turkey is heated through.

4. Gently stir in the cooked quinoa. Add the remaining stock if the mixture seems dry and check the seasoning. Cook for 2 minutes to heat through. Garnish with parsley and serve immediately.

NEW POTATO PIZZA WITH SPINACH & PANCETTA

SERVES: 2

PREP TIME: 40 MINS PLUS RISING

COOK TIME: 25 MINS

INGREDIENTS

1 (6-ounce) package baby spinach, coarsely chopped

3 tablespoons olive oil, plus extra for oiling

10 ounces new potatoes, unpeeled, cooked and sliced

2 cups shredded Gruyère or Swiss cheese

1 tablespoon chopped fresh rosemary leaves

2 ounces thinly sliced pancetta, cut into small pieces

salt and pepper, to taste

PIZZA CRUST

1 cup white bread flour

1 cup all-purpose flour

1 teaspoon salt

1 teaspoon active dry yeast

½ – ⅔ cup lukewarm water

1. To make the pizza crust, sift the dry ingredients into a bowl. Make a well in the center, pour in the water, and stir to a coarse dough. Gather into a ball and knead for 10–15 minutes, until smooth. Place in an oiled bowl, turning to coat. Cover with plastic wrap and let rise in a warm place for 1½–2 hours, until doubled in size.

2. Preheat the oven to 475°F. Oil a pizza pan. Blanch the spinach in a large saucepan of boiling water for 10 seconds. Drain and rinse under cold running water, squeezing out as much liquid as possible. Separate into small clumps.

3. Heat the oil in a large skillet. Add the potatoes and sauté for 3–4 minutes, turning, until lightly browned. Drain on paper towels.

4. Roll out the dough into a 12-inch circle. Place on the prepared pan. Sprinkle with 1¼ cups of the shredded cheese and arrange the potato slices on top. Sprinkle with the rosemary and season with salt and pepper. Arrange the spinach over the potatoes. Sprinkle with the remaining cheese and the pancetta.

5. Bake in the preheated oven for 10–15 minutes, turning the pan halfway through so the front is at the back, until bubbling. Serve immediately.

PORK-STUFFED LEAVES

SERVES: 4   **PREP TIME: 45 MINS**   **COOK TIME: 1 HR**

INGREDIENTS

1 tablespoon olive oil

1 tablespoon butter

1 (14½-ounce) can diced tomatoes

2 cups chicken stock or vegetable stock

1 onion, grated

8 large cabbage or collard greens leaves, thick stalks removed

12 ounces fresh ground pork

½ cup cooked white rice

finely grated zest of 1 lemon

2 teaspoons paprika

½ teaspoon dill seeds or caraway seeds

1 egg, lightly beaten

salt and pepper, to taste

chopped fresh dill, to garnish

1. Heat the oil and butter in a large skillet. Add the tomatoes, stock, and all but 2 tablespoons of the grated onion. Season with salt and pepper. Bring to a boil, then reduce the heat and simmer gently while you prepare the leaves.

2. Bring a large saucepan of water to a boil. Add the leaves and blanch for 2 minutes. Drain and rinse under cold running water, then pat dry.

3. Combine the pork, rice, lemon zest, paprika, dill seeds, egg, and the remaining onion. Add ¾ teaspoon salt and ¼ teaspoon pepper and mix well. Divide the stuffing among the leaves. Fold over the bottom edge and sides of each leaf, then roll up to make a package.

4. Place the packages, seam-side down, in the sauce. Cover and simmer over low heat for 45 minutes, until cooked through.

5. Sprinkle with fresh dill and serve immediately.

HERO TIPS

Make sure you use a skillet large enough to take the packages in a single layer, but not so large that they can slide around and unroll.

GROW YOUR OWN

There are few greater pleasures than growing your own greens, harvesting them as and when you need to, and knowing that what you are eating is absolutely fresh. You also get to try cultivars and varieties that aren't normally available in the stores.

WHAT TO GROW

There is an exciting choice in the seed catalogs, and it's easy to get carried away. It's a good idea to whittle down your options by asking yourself the following questions:

1. How much space do I have?

If room is limited, remember that a surprising number of greens can be grown in potting mix-filled flowerpots. Use your imagination—old buckets, sinks, and trash cans are all possibilities. Window boxes are good, too, especially for salad greens.

2. How much time do I have?

Don't bother with cabbages, baby broccoli, and Brussels sprouts if you're pushed for time. They take months to mature, and caterpillars love them. Go for fast and reliable croppers so you can enjoy the results of your labor in a few weeks.

3. What do I like to eat?

It's pointless growing spinach or Brussels sprouts if you or your family dislike them. However, if you enjoy eating salads, growing your own lettuce could save you a fortune.

THE PICK OF THE CROP
Salad greens

Salad greens are speedy growers and you can experiment with interesting cultivars rarely seen in the stores.

Arugula is a must. Flavorwise it beats store-bought arugula, it's really easy to grow, and will usually reseed itself, giving you a long supply of tasty, peppery leaves.

There is a huge choice of lettuce. It's a good idea to experiment with a packet of mixed seeds so that you can see which lettuce grow best in your soil. The beauty of lettuce is that you can harvest it at any stage, even as fledgling seedlings. Use the thinnings to sprinkle over salads or to garnish other dishes. The leaves of nonhearting lettuces can be cut at ground level and more will grow. Sow a little and often, and keep a vigilant eye out for snails and slugs.

Swiss chard

One of the most rewarding greens to grow, Swiss chard is resistant to pests and diseases, comes with a choice of colorful stems, and will last most of the year without bolting. It can be harvested whole, or as a cut-and-come-again crop—remove individual leaves as you need them and more will grow.

Perpetual spinach

Also known as spinach beet, this beginner-friendly plant is perfect for small spaces. As the name suggests, keep harvesting the leaves and more will grow. It will crop prolifically throughout the year and, with luck, the following year.

Bok choy

Shallow-rooted and ideal for containers, bok choy grows in cooler weather—a welcome sight when other greens are thin on the ground. Keep the crop going by harvesting leaves from the outside, or cutting whole heads just above ground level and leaving them to resprout.

TUNA WITH BOK CHOY & SOBA NOODLES

SERVES: 2   **PREP TIME: 25 MINS**   **COOK TIME: 20 MINS**

INGREDIENTS

1 pound bok choy

4 ounces soba noodles

2 (6-ounce) tuna steaks, about ⅝ inch thick

2 tablespoons peanut oil, plus extra for brushing

2 slices fresh ginger, cut into matchsticks

½–1 fresh red chile, seeded and thinly sliced

4 scallions, some green included, thickly sliced diagonally

1 cup frozen edamame (soybeans), thawed

2 tablespoons chicken stock, vegetable stock, or water

squeeze of lime juice

3 tablespoons chopped fresh cilantro

sea salt and pepper, to taste

1. Slice the bok choy stems into bite-size pieces. Slice the leaves into wide ribbons.

2. Bring a large saucepan of lightly salted water to a boil. Add the noodles, bring back to a boil, and cook for 5–6 minutes, until just tender. Drain, reserving the cooking water. Rinse well and set aside. Return the reserved water to the pan and keep warm over low heat.

3. Meanwhile, cut the tuna steaks into thirds. Brush with oil and season with sea salt and pepper. Heat a ridged grill pan over high heat. Add the tuna and cook for 2–2½ minutes on each side. Transfer to a plate and set aside in a warm place.

4. Heat a wok over medium–high heat. Add the oil and sauté the ginger, chile, and scallions for a few seconds.

5. Add the bok choy stems, edamame, and stock and stir-fry for 3 minutes. Add the bok choy leaves and stir-fry for an additional minute. Add the lime juice and cilantro, then season with sea salt and pepper.

6. Reheat the noodles in the cooking water, then drain. Divide the noodles between two plates, add the vegetables, and arrange the tuna on top. Serve immediately.

RADICCHIO & SHRIMP RISOTTO

SERVES: 3-4   **PREP TIME:** 15 MINS   **COOK TIME:** 35 MINS
                                                          PLUS RESTING

INGREDIENTS

½ head of radicchio
¼ cup olive oil
4 tablespoons butter
2 shallots, finely chopped
2 cups risotto rice
½ cup white wine
3 cups hot chicken stock
2 tablespoons lemon juice,
plus extra to taste
½ cup freshly grated
Parmesan cheese
8 ounces raw jumbo shrimp,
peeled and deveined
salt and pepper, to taste
fresh basil leaves, to garnish

1. Remove the thick stems from the radicchio and slice the leaves widthwise into ribbons.

2. Heat half the oil with half the butter in a large skillet over medium heat. Add the shallots and sauté for 5 minutes, until soft but not browned. Add the rice, stirring to coat the grains. Pour in the wine and stir until absorbed.

3. Add the stock, a ladleful at a time, stirring until each addition is absorbed before adding the next, until the rice is tender but still firm to the bite. When almost all the stock has been absorbed, stir in all but a handful of the radicchio, the lemon juice, Parmesan, and the remaining butter. Season with salt and pepper, then remove from the heat, cover, and let rest for 5 minutes.

4. Meanwhile, heat the remaining oil in a skillet over medium–high heat. Add the shrimp and cook for 4–5 minutes, until pink. Season with salt, pepper, and lemon juice.

5. Top the risotto with the shrimp and the remaining radicchio leaves. Garnish with basil leaves and serve immediately.

A LITTLE ON THE SIDE

ROASTED KALE CHIPS

Kale's meaty flavor becomes wonderfully intense when the leaves are roasted. Torn into bite-size pieces, they make crispy morsels that are perfect served with drinks or sprinkled over soup.

SERVES: 4   **PREP TIME: 15 MINS**   **COOK TIME: 15 MINS**

INGREDIENTS

8 ounces kale
(about 3 cups prepared)
2 tablespoons olive oil
2 pinches of sugar
2 pinches of sea salt
2 tablespoons toasted slivered
almonds, to garnish

1. Preheat the oven to 300°F. Remove the thick stems and main rib from the kale. Rinse and dry thoroughly with paper towels. Tear into bite-size pieces and place in a bowl with the oil and sugar, then toss well.

2. Spread about half the leaves in a single layer in a large roasting pan, spaced well apart. Sprinkle with a pinch of sea salt and roast on the bottom shelf of the preheated oven for 4 minutes.

3. Stir the leaves, then turn the pan so the back is at the front. Roast for an additional 1–2 minutes, until the leaves are crisp and slightly browned at the edges. Repeat with the remaining leaves and sea salt. Sprinkle the kale chips with the slivered almonds and serve immediately.

HERO TIPS

It's important to put the roasting pan on the bottom shelf of the oven where the heat is gentler. The leaves can easily burn, so check them often.

ROASTED BROCCOLI WITH PINE NUTS & PARMESAN

SERVES: 4   **PREP TIME: 20 MINS**   **COOK TIME: 25 MINS**

INGREDIENTS

1 large head of broccoli, in one piece
⅓ cup olive oil
1 teaspoon sea salt
¼ teaspoon pepper
¼ cup toasted pine nuts
grated zest of ½ lemon
1 ounce Parmesan cheese shavings
lemon wedges, to garnish

1. Preheat the oven to 450°F. Cut off the broccoli crown where it meets the stems. Remove the outer peel from the stem. Slice the stem widthwise into 3¼-inch pieces, then quarter each slice lengthwise. Cut the crown into 1½-inch-wide wedges.

2. Put the broccoli wedges and stems into a bowl. Sprinkle with the oil, sea salt, and pepper, gently tossing to coat. Spread out in a large roasting pan. Cover tightly with aluminum foil and roast on the bottom shelf of the preheated oven for 10 minutes.

3. Remove the foil, then roast for an additional 5–8 minutes, until just starting to brown. Turn the stems and wedges over, and roast for an additional 3–5 minutes, until tender.

4. Transfer to a shallow, warm serving dish along with any cooking juices. Sprinkle with the pine nuts and lemon zest, tossing to mix. Sprinkle the Parmesan shavings over the top.

5. Garnish with lemon wedges and serve hot, warm or at room temperature.

STIR-FRIED BRUSSELS SPROUTS WITH ALMONDS

SERVES: 4   **PREP TIME: 20 MINS**   **COOK TIME: 15 MINS**

INGREDIENTS

1 pound Brussels sprouts, outer leaves and stems removed (about 5 cups)

2 tablespoons peanut oil

1 tablespoon toasted sesame oil

1 shallot, finely chopped

1¼-inch piece fresh ginger, finely chopped

1 garlic clove, thinly sliced

3–4 tablespoons chicken stock or vegetable stock

juice of ½ lime

3 tablespoons unskinned almonds, halved lengthwise

¼ cup chopped fresh cilantro

salt and pepper, to taste

lime wedges, to garnish

1. Bring a large saucepan of water to a boil. Add the Brussels sprouts and blanch for 3 minutes. Drain and rinse under cold running water, then pat dry with paper towels. Slice lengthwise into quarters.

2. Heat a wok or large skillet over medium–high heat. Add the peanut oil and sesame oil. Add the shallot, ginger, and garlic and stir-fry for 1–2 minutes, or until the garlic is just starting to color.

3. Add the sprouts, stock, and lime juice. Season with salt and pepper, then stir-fry for 2–3 minutes, until the sprouts are beginning to soften. Stir in the almonds and stir-fry for 1–2 minutes, or until the sprouts are tender but still bright green.

4. Stir in the cilantro, garnish with lime wedges, and serve immediately.

HERO TIPS

Be careful not to overcook the Brussels sprouts in step 1, otherwise they will absorb too much water and become soggy.

SPICY BOK CHOY WITH SESAME SAUCE

Bok choy, also known as pak choi, is a member of the cabbage family. Popular in Asian cooking, here it is stir-fried with chile and garlic and drizzled with a tasty sesame sauce.

SERVES: 4　　　　**PREP TIME: 20 MINS**　　　**COOK TIME: 10 MINS**

INGREDIENTS

5 small heads of bok choy

2 teaspoons peanut or vegetable oil

1 fresh red chile, seeded and thinly sliced

1 garlic clove, thinly sliced

½ cup vegetable stock

SAUCE

2½ tablespoons sesame seeds

2 tablespoons dark soy sauce

2 teaspoons packed light brown sugar

1 garlic clove, crushed

3 tablespoons sesame oil

1. For the sesame sauce, toast the sesame seeds in a dry skillet over medium heat, stirring until lightly browned. Remove from the heat and cool slightly. Transfer to a mortar. Add the soy sauce, sugar, and crushed garlic and pound to a coarse paste with a pestle. Stir in the sesame oil.

2. Quarter the bok choy lengthwise and set aside.

3. Heat the peanut oil in a wok or large skillet. Add the chile and sliced garlic, and stir-fry for 20–30 seconds. Add the bok choy and stir-fry for 5 minutes, adding the stock, a little at a time, to prevent them from sticking.

4. Transfer the bok choy to a warm serving dish, drizzle the sesame sauce over them, and serve immediately.

HERO TIPS

When selecting your bok choy for this recipe, choose small ones that have perky leaves and unblemished stems.

BABY BROCCOLI WITH CAPER BUTTER SAUCE

SERVES: 4   **PREP TIME: 15 MINS**   **COOK TIME: 20 MINS**

INGREDIENTS

1½ pounds baby broccoli

3 tablespoons extra virgin olive oil

3 shallots, thinly sliced

2 large garlic cloves, thinly sliced

pinch of crushed red pepper flakes

3 tablespoons toasted pine nuts

4 tablespoons butter

2 tablespoons capers, drained

¼ cup snipped fresh chives

1 ounce Parmesan cheese shavings

salt and pepper, to taste

cooked pasta, to serve

1. Cut off the broccoli florets and slice lengthwise if thick. Slice the leaves and stems into ¾-inch pieces. Steam over a saucepan of boiling water for 2 minutes, until barely soft. Remove from the heat and reserve the cooking water.

2. Heat the oil in a large skillet over low–medium heat. Add the shallots and sauté for 5 minutes. Add the garlic and sauté for 2–3 minutes, until just starting to brown.

3. Increase the heat to medium and add the broccoli. Add the red pepper flakes and season with salt and pepper. Add 3–4 tablespoons of the reserved broccoli cooking water. Cook, stirring, for 4–6 minutes, until the broccoli is just tender and still bright green.

4. Stir in the pine nuts and check the seasoning, adding salt and pepper. Transfer to a serving dish and keep warm.

5. Heat a heavy skillet. When hot, add the butter and sizzle until golden. Remove from the heat and stir in the capers and half the chives.

6. Pour the sauce over the broccoli. Sprinkle with the Parmesan shavings and the remaining chives. Serve immediately with pasta.

WHAT'S COOKING?

The rule of thumb when cooking greens is a short cooking time for crispness and color, or long, slow cooking to bring out sweetness. If you go for the short method, remember that greens continue to cook after they have been removed from the heat.

ROASTING

Roasting is an excellent way to cook broccoli florets, or bite-size pieces of kale or Swiss chard. The dry heat of the oven caramelizes their natural sugars, resulting in full-on meaty flavors. Roast at a high temperature and don't overcrowd the pan.

BOILING

There are two schools of thought about boiling: one is to use a minimum amount of water so there is less liquid for vitamins to leach into; the other is to use a large volume of already boiling water, the advantage being speed and, therefore, better color and texture. Regardless of method, it's a good idea to boil greens uncovered, otherwise acids in the steam will gather under the lid and drip onto the leaves, changing the color to a drab olive green. To prevent red cabbage from turning blue, add a little lemon juice or vinegar to the cooking water. If you are boiling spinach, there is no need to add extra water—there will be enough left on the leaves from washing and they will also eventually release their own moisture.

STEAMING

Steaming is ideal for porous greens, such as broccoli, spinach, Brussels sprouts, and some types of cabbage. The vegetables are not in direct contact with the liquid, so they don't become waterlogged. They retain more flavor this way and keep their vibrant colors.

FRYING

Gentle pan-frying is a great way of wilting tender greens, such as baby spinach, young Swiss chard, or arugula, before adding them to dishes such as pasta or risotto. Larger, sturdier greens, such as cabbage or kale, usually need blanching in boiling water to soften them before frying or stir-frying. Stir-frying in hot oil is easy, speedy, and ideal for leafy greens, especially bok choy and napa cabbage. The stems take longer to cook, so slice them thinly and cook them first before adding the leaves. If you are adding greens to a mixed stir-fry, add the stems along with other vegetables, such as carrots and onion. Stir in the leaves at the end.

BRAISING

Braising is a gentle way of cooking sturdy greens, such as kale, cabbage, and collard greens. Soften the greens first by gently sautéing them with onion and other seasonings, then finish cooking in a covered dish with just enough water or stock to produce steam while cooking. The leaves produce their own juices, resulting in a mouthwatering dish of tender, flavor-packed greens.

BRAISED PEAS WITH LETTUCE & TARRAGON

SERVES: 4   PREP TIME: 10 MINS   COOK TIME: 15 MINS

INGREDIENTS:

1 tablespoon butter
1 tablespoon olive oil
1 leek, thinly sliced
2 teaspoons all-purpose flour
1 cup vegetable stock
2½ cups fresh or frozen peas
2 butterhead lettuce, sliced
3 tablespoons chopped fresh tarragon
1 tablespoon lemon juice
salt and pepper, to taste

1. Heat the butter and oil in a large saucepan. Add the leek, cover, and cook over low heat for 5 minutes, until soft. Stir in the flour, then gradually stir in the stock.

2. Add the peas, increase the heat, cover, and simmer for 4 minutes. Add the lettuce without stirring it in, cover, and simmer for an additional 2 minutes, until the vegetables are tender.

3. Stir in the lettuce, tarragon, and lemon juice. Season with salt and pepper and serve immediately.

HERO TIPS

To vary the flavor, replace the tarragon with mint, or the lettuce with Belgian endive.

SPICY GREENS WITH BLACK BEANS & ORANGES

This colorful dish is equally delicious made with kale or collard greens. The emerald leaves look stunning with black beans and orange, and the full-bodied flavor of the greens is a good match for the chile and garlic.

SERVES: 4   **PREP TIME: 25 MINS**   **COOK TIME: 25 MINS**

INGREDIENTS

1 large orange

3 tablespoons olive oil, plus extra for drizzling

1 small onion, finely chopped

1 garlic clove, finely chopped

1 fresh green chile, seeded and finely chopped

1¼ pounds kale, thick stems removed and leaves sliced widthwise (about 8½ cups) or 1¼ pounds collard greens, trimmed and sliced (about 20 cups)

⅓–½ cup vegetable stock or chicken stock

1 (15-ounce) can black beans, drained and rinsed

⅓ cup chopped fresh cilantro

1. Using a sharp knife, cut a slice from the top and bottom of the orange. Remove the peel and white pith by cutting downward, following the shape of the fruit as closely as possible. Working over a bowl, cut between the flesh and membrane of each segment and ease out the flesh. Slice each segment in half. Squeeze the membrane over the bowl to extract the juice.

2. Heat the oil in a large skillet over medium heat. Add the onion and sauté for 5 minutes, until soft. Add the garlic and chile and sauté for an additional 2 minutes.

3. Gradually stir in the kale or collard greens. Add a splash of stock, then cover and cook for 5–6 minutes, or until wilted. Add more stock if the leaves start to look dry. Stir in the orange juice and any remaining stock. Season with salt and pepper, then cover and cook for 5 minutes, until tender.

4. Stir in the beans and the orange segments. Simmer, uncovered, for a few minutes to heat through. Stir in the cilantro, drizzle with a little oil, and serve immediately.

STEAMED GREENS WITH LEMON & CILANTRO

This simple dish of lightly steamed crisp cabbage and velvety baby spinach is brought to life with a citrusy hit of lemon, aromatic fresh cilantro, and biting black pepper.

SERVES: 4   **PREP TIME: 15 MINS**   **COOK TIME: 10 MINS**

INGREDIENTS

1 head of spring cabbage, tough outer leaves discarded

1 (6-ounce) package baby spinach

large pat of unsalted butter

finely grated zest of ½ lemon

¼ cup chopped fresh cilantro

sea salt and pepper

1. Cut the cabbage in quarters lengthwise and cut out the tough stem. Slice the quarters widthwise into ¾-inch ribbons. Steam for 3 minutes, until starting to soften.

2. Arrange the spinach on top of the cabbage and steam for an additional 3 minutes. Drain in a colander to remove any excess liquid.

3. Transfer the cabbage and spinach to a warm serving dish. Stir in the butter, lemon zest, and cilantro, mixing well.

4. Sprinkle with sea salt and pepper and serve immediately.

BABY BROCCOLI WITH ROASTED SQUASH SAUCE

SERVES: 4   PREP TIME: 30 MINS   COOK TIME: 50 MINS

INGREDIENTS

½ kabocha squash
1 small onion, halved lengthwise
1 large garlic clove, unpeeled
oil, for brushing
1½ tablespoons tahini
2 teaspoons soy sauce
squeeze of lemon juice
1 pound baby broccoli, trimmed
pat of butter
salt and pepper, to taste

1. Preheat the oven to 400°F. Cut the squash into wedges and remove the seeds, but do not peel.

2. Place the squash in a roasting pan and tightly cover with aluminum foil. Roast in the preheated oven for 35–40 minutes, until tender.

3. Meanwhile, put the onion and garlic into a separate small roasting pan and brush with oil. Roast, uncovered, for 20 minutes, or until the onion just begins to brown.

4. Peel the squash and garlic, then put the flesh into a food processor with the onion and process to a thick puree. Scrape the puree into a saucepan. Whisk in the tahini, soy sauce, and lemon juice and season with salt and pepper.

5. Cut off the broccoli florets and thickly slice the stems. Steam the broccoli stems and florets for 5–7 minutes, until tender but still bright green. Reserve the cooking water. Transfer the broccoli to a warm serving dish and keep warm.

6. Use some of the broccoli cooking water to thin the squash sauce to a thick pouring consistency. Reheat over low heat, then stir in the butter and season with salt and pepper.

7. Pour the sauce over the broccoli and serve immediately.

BRUSSELS SPROUT & RED CABBAGE SLAW

SERVES: 4

PREP TIME: 20 MINS PLUS STANDING

COOK TIME: 5 MINS PLUS COOLING

INGREDIENTS

8 ounces Brussels sprouts, outer leaves and stems removed (about 4 cups)

¼ head of red cabbage

½ teaspoon salt

½ cup pecans

⅓ cup dried cranberries

6 scallions, some green included, sliced diagonally

⅓ cup fresh flat-leaf parsley leaves

1½ cups cress, radish sprouts, or alfafa sprouts

DRESSING

2 teaspoons honey

1½ teaspoons lemon juice

¼ teaspoon Dijon mustard

¼ cup cold-pressed canola oil or walnut oil

1. Cut the Brussels sprouts into quarters, discard the cores, and slice the leaves widthwise into thin shreds.

2. Remove the outer leaves and core of the red cabbage. Slice lengthwise into three segments, then slice the segments widthwise into thin shreds.

3. Put the sprouts and cabbage into a serving bowl and sprinkle with the salt. Toss with your hands, then set aside for 30 minutes to soften slightly.

4. Meanwhile, preheat the oven to 300°F. Put the pecans in a small baking pan and toast in the preheated oven for 4–5 minutes. Let cool, then slice in half.

5. Add the pecans, cranberries, scallions, and parsley to the Brussels sprouts and cabbage, gently tossing to mix.

6. To make the dressing, whisk together all the ingredients in a small bowl. Pour over the salad and gently toss. Sprinkle the cress or sprouts over the top. Let stand at room temperature for 30 minutes before serving to let the flavors develop.

SALAD OF MIXED GREENS & HERBS

This simple salad relies on contrasting colors and flavors. Deep green watercress, yellow-green frisée, and ruby red mustard leaves are a great combination with tiny bok choy leaves and soft leafy herbs.

SERVES: 4　　　**PREP TIME: 20 MINS**　　　**COOK TIME: NONE**

INGREDIENTS

8 scallions

2 cups watercress or arugula

2 cups frisée

1 cup red mustard leaves, torn into bite-size pieces

small handful of baby bok choy or baby kale leaves

small handful of fresh soft-leaf herbs, such as basil, mint, cilantro, and flat-leaf parsley

large pinch of sea salt

3–4 tablespoons hazelnut oil

1 tablespoon rice vinegar or white wine vinegar

½ cup toasted hazelnuts, coarsely chopped

1. Trim the scallions, keeping some of the green. Slice lengthwise into 1-inch strips.

2. Put the watercress, frisée, red mustard leaves, bok choy, herbs, and scallions into a large salad bowl. Sprinkle with the sea salt. Toss gently with your hands to distribute the salt.

3. Pour in enough of the oil barely to coat the leaves and gently toss. Add the vinegar and toss again.

4. Sprinkle the hazelnuts over the top and serve immediately.

FRISÉE SALAD WITH WALNUT OIL DRESSING

SERVES: 4   PREP TIME: 10 MINS   COOK TIME: 5 MINS
                                                  PLUS COOLING

INGREDIENTS

½ head of frisée, leaves separated and torn into bite-size pieces

1 romaine lettuce heart, leaves separated and torn into bite-size pieces

DRESSING

½ cup walnut pieces, larger pieces broken up

3 tablespoons olive oil

1 teaspoon honey

1 tablespoon white wine vinegar

1 teaspoon Dijon mustard

pepper, to taste

1. First, make the dressing. Put the walnuts in a skillet, add 1 tablespoon of the oil, and cook over medium heat for 2–3 minutes, or until lightly toasted. Remove from the heat, drizzle with the honey, and stir; the heat from the pan will be enough to caramelize the mixture slightly.

2. Add the remaining oil to the pan and stir, then let cool for 15 minutes so the walnuts flavor the oil. When it is cool, put the vinegar and mustard into a small bowl, season with a little pepper, and beat together, then stir into the walnuts and oil.

3. Put the frisée and romaine in a salad bowl. Spoon the dressing over them, toss gently, and serve immediately.

HERO TIPS

It's important to dry the leaves well after washing, otherwise the dressing won't cling to them. Use a salad spinner, then spread out the leaves on paper towels to blot up excess moisture. After adding the dressing, toss the salad gently with your hands.

RAINBOW SALAD WITH WASABI DRESSING

A salad doesn't need to be complicated to be good. This simple but delicious salad is an interesting way to present rainbow Swiss chard with its beautifully colored stems and contrasting leaves.

SERVES: 4   **PREP TIME: 10 MINS**   **COOK TIME: 5 MINS PLUS COOLING**

INGREDIENTS

1 tablespoon sunflower oil
¼ cup sunflower seeds
2 tablespoons soy sauce
8 ounces rainbow Swiss chard

DRESSING

1 teaspoon wasabi paste
1 tablespoon mirin
juice of 1 small orange
pepper, to taste

1. Heat the oil in a lidded skillet over medium heat. Add the sunflower seeds, cover with the lid, and cook for 2–3 minutes, shaking the pan so they don't stick, until you hear them begin to pop. Remove the pan from the heat, add the soy sauce, cover with the lid again, and let cool.

2. To make the dressing, put the wasabi paste, mirin, orange juice, and a little pepper in a clean screw-top jar, screw on the lid, and shake well.

3. Chop the Swiss chard stems into chunks and slice the leaves into ribbons. Put in a salad bowl, drizzle with the dressing, and toss gently. Sprinkle with the toasted sunflower seeds and serve immediately.

GREEN JUICES

LETTUCE & KIWI QUENCHER

Jewel-like kiwis and juicy green grapes are blended with naturally sweet pear in this thirst-busting drink. Lettuce is perfect to include in a juice because it is about 90 percent water.

SERVES: 1 **PREP TIME: 10 MINS** **COOK TIME: NONE**

INGREDIENTS

½ romaine lettuce
4 kiwis, peeled
¾ cup green grapes
1 large pear, halved
small handful of ice, to serve (optional)

1. Peel off a lettuce leaf and reserve for decoration.

2. Feed the kiwis and grapes through a juicer, followed by the lettuce and pear.

3. Fill a glass halfway with ice (if using), then pour in the juice.

4. Decorate with the reserved lettuce leaf and serve immediately.

KALE & MANGO JUICE

This pretty green-speckled drink looks mango-free, but the mango's flavor comes through even if its color is disguised. The natural sweetness of the mango balances the strong taste of the kale.

SERVES: 1 **PREP TIME: 10 MINS** **COOK TIME: NONE**

INGREDIENTS

1 tablespoon sesame seeds
juice of ½ lime
1 cup torn kale pieces
1 mango, peeled, pitted, and coarsely chopped
1 cup unsweetened soy milk
small handful of crushed ice

1. Put the sesame seeds in a blender or food processor and process until finely ground.

2. Add the lime juice, kale, and mango to the blender and process again.

3. Add the soy milk and crushed ice and process until smooth.

4. Pour into a glass and serve immediately.

HERO TIPS

With its high calcium content from the sesame seeds, kale, and fortified soy milk, this juice will be good for your bones. Make sure that you grind the sesame seeds to a fine powder before adding the other ingredients.

SPINACH & MELON COOLER

This cleansing juice is a healthy alternative to sugar-laden commercially made drinks. The sweet and juicy melon balances out the stronger taste of the spinach, and the parsley and mint add extra zing.

SERVES: 1   **PREP TIME: 10 MINS**   **COOK TIME: NONE**

INGREDIENTS

½ Galia or honeydew melon, peeled and thickly sliced

3 cups baby spinach

2 large stems of fresh flat-leaf parsley

3 large stems of fresh mint

small handful of ice (optional)

1. Feed the melon through a juicer, followed by the spinach, parsley, and two stems of the mint.

2. Fill a glass halfway with ice (if using), then pour in the juice.

3. Decorate with the remaining stem of mint and serve immediately.

HERO TIPS

There's no need to remove the seeds from the melon, because the juicer will make speedy work of separating them out.

GO FOR JUICE!

Most of us know that green vegetables are packed with health-promoting vitamins and minerals. They contain significant amounts of vitamin C and folate—a type of B vitamin needed by pregnant women and growing children—and essential minerals, such as calcium and iron. What we may not know, however, is that green vegetables are mostly water—about 75 to 90 percent—and this makes them ideal candidates for juicing.

Drinking their juice is a convenient and instant way of getting all that goodness directly into your system. That said, vegetable juice shouldn't replace the vegetables you eat at mealtimes. Drink it as an accompaniment to a meal, or as an energy-boosting breakfast or snack.

If certain green vegetables are a challenge to eat, you'll find the juice slips down more easily. Because green vegetables contain hardly any sugar, they won't make your energy levels fluctuate in the same way as fruit and sweeter vegetables, such as carrots and beets, do. Add these to balance out the flavor of the juice, but limit them to no more than one-third of the total juice.

Juicing can be time-consuming and may take a while to become a habit. Advance preparation certainly helps. If you're planning on drinking juice for breakfast, it's a good idea to select the produce the night before, wash it carefully, and have the juicer set up and ready to go.

If you're new to green vegetable juice, start off with mildly flavored romaine or iceberg lettuce, perhaps blended with an apple or carrot. You can then move on to spinach, Swiss chard, napa cabbage, or crunchy bok choy. For extra depth of flavor, add a small slice of lemon, a garlic clove, or a slice of fresh ginger. If the flavor is too strong, dilute the juice with mineral water. Strongest of all are broccoli, kale, and cabbage. Their powerful flavors need taming with a sweeter fruit or vegetable, such as apple, celery, cucumber, fennel or carrot.

Vegetable juice is highly perishable. Once exposed to light, heat, and air, the nutrients are partly destroyed, so it should be drunk right away. If you have to store your juice, put it in a sealed container in the refrigerator for no more than 24 hours.

BROCCOLI & PARSLEY REVITALIZER

Wonderfully soothing and gentle, this delicate, reviving green juice is naturally sweet and refreshing, and makes a perfect alternative to a caffeine-loaded tea or coffee in the afternoon.

SERVES: 1   **PREP TIME: 10 MINS**   **COOK TIME: NONE**

INGREDIENTS

1½ cups large broccoli florets

small handful of fresh flat-leaf parsley

½ fennel bulb

2 apples, halved

chilled water, to taste (optional)

small handful of ice (optional)

1. Feed the broccoli and parsley through the juicer, followed by the fennel and apples.

2. Fill up the juice with chilled water to taste, if desired.

3. Fill a glass halfway with ice (if using), then pour in the juice. Serve immediately.

HERO TIPS

There's no need to add water to the juice if you don't want to—it depends on how thirsty you are and how strong the juice tastes.

ARUGULA, APPLE & GINSENG REFRESHER

Arugula has a peppery flavor, so if you're new to green juices, then this might not be the one to start you off. Ginseng is a natural stimulant that helps to combat stress and lifts the mood.

SERVES: 1   **PREP TIME: 10 MINS**   **COOK TIME: NONE**

INGREDIENTS

1 ginseng tea bag or
1 teaspoon ginseng tea
⅔ cup boiling water
1 apple, halved
1½ cups arugula

1. Put the tea bag in a cup, pour in the boiling water, and let steep for 4 minutes. Strain the tea into a glass.

2. Feed the apple through a juicer, followed by the arugula.

3. Stir the juice into the tea and serve warm.

HERO TIPS

This revitalizing drink can also be enjoyed cold. Simply let cool, then drop in some ice cubes and stir well before serving.

KALE, LETTUCE & AVOCADO JUICE

It would be easy to believe that just looking at this green drink could make you feel healthier! The good news is that it really is bursting with vitamins and minerals.

SERVES: 1   **PREP TIME: 10 MINS**   **COOK TIME: NONE**

INGREDIENTS

1 cup kale

small handful of fresh flat-leaf parsley

½ romaine lettuce

3 celery stalks, halved

1 apple, halved

½ lemon

⅓ cup slivered almonds

½ avocado, peeled and pitted

small handful of crushed ice (optional)

1. Feed the kale through a juicer, followed by the parsley and lettuce. Finally, feed two of the celery stalks, the apple, and lemon through the juicer.

2. Put the slivered almonds in a blender or food processor and process until finely ground.

3. Add the juice and avocado flesh to the almonds, and process until smooth. Add the crushed ice (if using) and blend again.

4. Pour the juice into a glass. Decorate with the remaining celery stalk and serve immediately.

SPINACH, WATERCRESS & ZUCCHINI BOOSTER

If you like spinach or watercress soup, you'll love this juice. You don't get a huge amount of juice from these green leaves, but what you do get is concentrated with antioxidants, minerals, and vitamins.

SERVES: 1   **PREP TIME: 10 MINS**   **COOK TIME: NONE**

INGREDIENTS

2 cups baby spinach
1 cup watercress
1 zucchini, halved
2 apples, halved
1 teaspoon wheatgrass powder (optional)
small handful of ice (optional)

1. Feed the spinach and watercress through a juicer, followed by the zucchini and apples.

2. Stir the wheatgrass powder (if using) into the juice.

3. Fill a glass halfway with ice (if using), then pour in the juice. Serve immediately.

HERO TIPS

Unless you have a masticating juicer, fresh wheatgrass can be difficult to juice. The powdered wheatgrass used in this recipe is easier to use, although it doesn't contain as much nutrition.

SPINACH, CUCUMBER & AVOCADO JUICE

This supersmooth green juice is packed with antioxidants, vitamins, and minerals. It would be a fantastic choice for breakfast, giving you an energy boost without making you feel heavy.

SERVES: 1　　　　**PREP TIME: 10 MINS**　　　　**COOK TIME: NONE**

INGREDIENTS

1 pear, halved

¼ cucumber, coarsely chopped

1½ cups baby spinach

4 stems of fresh flat-leaf parsley

½ avocado, peeled and pitted

½ teaspoon spirulina powder

chilled water

1 Brazil nut, coarsely chopped

1. Feed the pear and cucumber through a juicer.

2. Pour the juice into a blender or food processor, then add the spinach, parsley, and avocado and blend until smooth. Pour the juice into a glass.

3. Mix the spirulina powder with just enough chilled water to make a thick liquid, then swirl it into the juice.

4. Sprinkle with the chopped Brazil nut, then serve immediately.

HERO TIPS

Look for packages of spirulina powder in health-food stores. This fine, white powder turns a dark shade of green when mixed with water. Made from a cultivated algae, it's a great protein booster.

Index

JUV/E   Smith, Maggie,
FIC   1965-

         Argo, you lucky dog.

$15.00

DATE